Queen Iween's
Beautiful Butterflies

Irene T. Hunt, Author and Photographer
Timothy J. Hunt, Editor and Photographer

HℓN
Hunt for Nature Publishing
San Diego, California

www.HuntForNature.com

Irene T. Hunt

Special thanks to

Tim Hunt for loving silly ole me unconditionally!

My family and friends for their love, encouragement and support!

David F. Marriott, Ph.D. for sharing his knowledge and passion for butterflies!

The Monarch Program (www.monarchprogram.org) for its commitment and
dedication to butterfly research and education!

Susan Walker for her educational guidance and support!

Mark Whitbeck for contributing his beautiful monarch butterfly photographs!

Nate Robb for his creativity and illustrative talent!

***

Are you looking for other Queen Iween books? Visit www.HuntForNature.com.

Library of Congress Control Number: 2009912780
Summary: Queen Iween entertains and educates children on her butterfly friends and their life cycle.
ISBN #978-0-9843071-1-1
[1. Children 2. Butterflies 3. Photography 4. Nature]
First Edition: March 2010   10 9 8 7 6 5 4 3 2 1

H ℓ
ℑ N
Hunt for Nature Publishing
San Diego, California

For information about Hunt for Nature Publishing visit our website at
www.HuntForNature.com
or send an email to QueenIween@HuntForNature.com.

Queen Iween books are made in the U.S.A.

Queen Iween's Beautiful Butterflies

Contents

Butterflies

They float through
the air with their wings
spread wide

Catching a breeze for a nice
long ride

Each movement flowing like a
rising tide

If you're ready to learn,
let Queen Iween be
your guide.

Hello!
It's so nice to see you.
Welcome to my world of beauty
and fun.

Have you ever seen anything more
beautiful than a butterfly? They are
beautiful in so many ways.

There is beauty in their colorful,
delicate wings. There is beauty in the
way they glide through the air, and
land softly on flowers. What's most
important is the beauty that comes
from all the good things they do to
help others, like you and me.

Do you like to do good
things for others?
I do!

Do you know how butterflies help you and everyone else in the world?

Butterflies, along with other insects and birds, pollinate plants and flowers. Do you know why pollination is important? Pollination produces seeds which increases the number of flowers and plants in the world. More flowers and plants means more food for everyone to eat.

Do you know how pollination happens? It all starts with two little words, "I'm hungry!" I bet you say those two little words a lot, don't you?

When butterflies get hungry they need food and they need it fast, because it gives them the energy they need to fly!

Butterflies love flower juice, called nectar. They love it so much that they fly from flower to flower looking for it. As they land on each flower, pollen gets stuck on their body which they carry to all the other flowers they visit. This is how butterflies help. They carry pollen from one flower to another which helps pollinate plants and flowers.

I have so many other fun
things to tell you about butterflies!

Do you know that my butterfly friends can be
found everywhere in the world except ONE place?
Can you guess where that is? I'll give you a hint: It's so
cold there that your teeth will chatter. It is Antarctica!
That was a tough one. Did you get the answer right?

Do you know that my butterfly friends come in all different
colors, shapes, and sizes? Each butterfly is different in its
own way; that's what makes the world more colorful and
interesting. It works the same way with your friends as it
does with mine. Your friends come in different colors,
shapes, and sizes too, don't they? Can you tell me
about your friends? Who is the tallest? Who
has the biggest feet? Who has the most
freckles? And, who has the
curliest hair?

My butterfly friends look different from one another but they are also alike, just like your friends. Do you know how your friends are alike?

My butterfly friends are alike in a very special way. They all change shape four times in their life. Wow! Four times! It is called a complete metamorphosis. That's a big word, but it simply means that their bodies change shape. As you grow your body changes too, but not like a butterfly's body. When you turn the page you will see all the different forms a butterfly takes as it gets older. It is wonderful!

9

Can you follow my arrows? They walk you through the different stages a butterfly goes through. Let's start with Stage 1. It is an egg. Butterflies begin as an egg. Can you point to the egg?

Then, in Stage 2, the larva hatches from the egg. What does the larva look like? You are right. It looks like a caterpillar. A larva is a caterpillar! Stage 2 is the caterpillar stage.

Do you know what happens next? It is amazing! The caterpillar turns into a "pupa." Pupa is a funny word, isn't it? Can you say "pu pah"? Just hearing that word makes me giggle! A pupa is also called a chrysalis. In Stage 3 of a butterfly's life cycle it is a chrysalis.

Finally, in Stage 4, a beautiful butterfly emerges from its chrysalis. Those are the four stages all butterflies go through!

Complete Metamorphosis

Stage 1

Egg

A Butterfly's Life Cycle

(Monarch butterfly)

Stage 4

Adult (Butterfly)

Stage 2

Larva (Caterpillar)

Stage 3

Pupa (Chrysalis)

Are you ready to
learn more about butterflies?

Do you remember the first stage of
a butterfly's metamorphosis? You're right,
it's an egg. Female butterflies lay their eggs
on leaves. Some like to lay their eggs on the
underside of leaves and some like to use the top
of leaves. How do butterflies keep their eggs from
rolling off the leaves? Do you think they use glue?
If you said yes, you're kind of right. The female
butterfly knows how to make a sticky glue-like
substance that keeps the egg on the leaf. It isn't
the same type of glue you use though; she
makes it just for her eggs.

Inside each egg a baby caterpillar is growing.
Once it is ready it will leave the egg. It can
take anywhere from four days to two
weeks to develop. The warmer the
temperature outside, the
faster it will grow.

A Butterfly Egg

Female butterflies are very picky about the types of plants they lay their eggs on. They choose plants that their babies like to eat. This monarch butterfly is drinking nectar from a milkweed flower. She also lays her eggs on milkweed leaves.

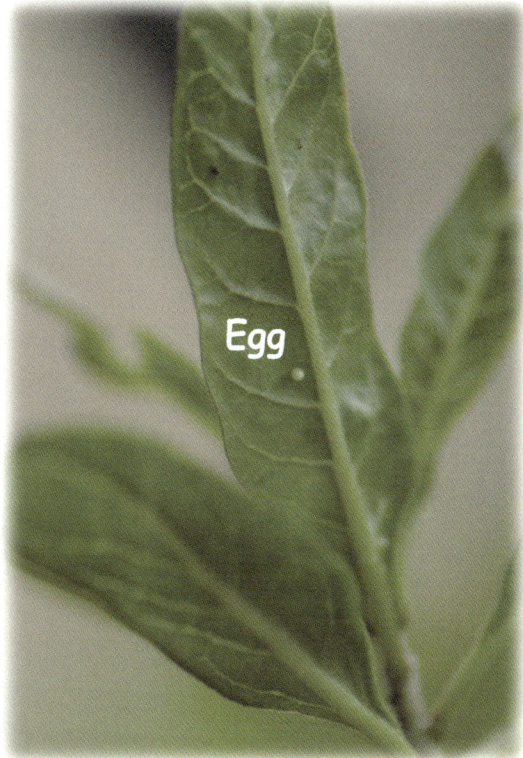

Egg

Can you see the egg? It is very tiny. A butterfly laid this egg on the underside of the leaf.

This is a close up picture of a monarch butterfly egg. The egg is much smaller than this picture.

If the egg is Stage 1, then what is Stage 2? That's right, it is the caterpillar stage.

Once the caterpillar hatches from the egg it becomes a **munching machine**. It eats and eats and eats some more! You might say that a caterpillar's life is spent at an all-you-can-eat buffet, because the only thing it does is eat. For almost three whole weeks it eats nonstop.

Caterpillars eat plants. Do you know what plant-eating creatures are called? It's another big word. They are called "herbivores." Each type of caterpillar has its own favorite food plants. Monarch caterpillars, for example, love to eat milkweed plants. Can you see the monarch caterpillar munching on the milkweed flower?

The more a caterpillar eats, the more it grows. In only three weeks caterpillars can grow to be almost 3,000 times bigger than they were when they left the egg. **Wow!** If you grew to be 3,000 times bigger than the day you were born you'd be as big as a GRAY WHALE! That's BIG!

2

To grow that big in such a short time caterpillars have to shed their skin four times. Each time they get too big for their skin they shed and grow again. Can you name other creatures that shed their skin?

Do you know why caterpillars need to shed their skin and you don't? It's because their skeleton is on the outside of their body and yours is on the inside. Can you see the caterpillar's skeleton? It's the skin that covers the outside of the caterpillar's body. It's called an "exoskeleton." Your skeleton is inside your body. It is called an "endoskeleton." You are so lucky! Your skeleton and skin grow as you grow.

A caterpillar

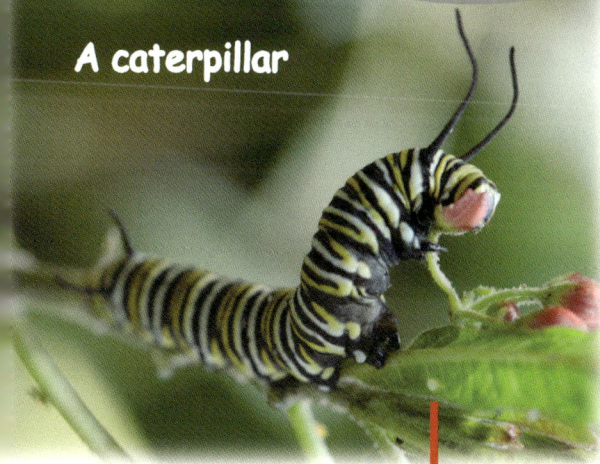

An egg

The more it eats, the more it grows! Look how much bigger the caterpillar is than the egg. Two to three weeks earlier it hatched from a tiny little egg, just like this one.

As the caterpillar grows larger it will need to shed to keep growing.

15

Caterpillars sure are
fun to look at!

Do you know how many legs a
caterpillar has? It has 16 legs.
At the front of its body it has six
"true legs," in the middle it has eight
"prolegs," and at the back it has
two "hind legs."

A caterpillar uses all of its legs for walking,
but some legs have other uses. The true
legs are also used for holding food,
and the prolegs are used for climbing.
Caterpillars are great climbers! They
have tiny rings at the bottom of their
prolegs that help them climb
straight up the stem of plants,
and upside down across
branches and leaves.

A Caterpillar's Body
Monarch Caterpillar (Larva)

Sound Sensors

Smell Sensors

Sound Sensors

Sound Sensors

Simple Eyes

2 Hind Legs

8 Prolegs

(for climbing)

6 True Legs

(for gripping food)

Caterpillars have six "simple" eyes on each side of their head. That's a lot of eyes! With all those eyes you would think they have great eyesight, but they do not. Their simple eyes only let them see changes in lighting, like shadows.

17

When the caterpillar is fully grown it finally stops eating and looks for a place where it can shed its skin for the last time.

In total, a caterpillar sheds its skin five times. The fifth time is when it enters the next stage of its life cycle. Can you remember the next stage? Think hard! Stage 3 is the chrysalis.

Once the caterpillar finds a branch or the underside of a leaf, it hangs upside down and sheds for the last time. As the caterpillar sheds it becomes a chrysalis.

Chrysalis (Pupa) Stage
Monarch Chrysalis

This caterpillar is getting ready to shed for the last time to become a chrysalis.

A chrysalis is kind of like a dressing room where caterpillars go to change into their butterfly clothes. That's a funny thought, isn't it? It's not quite as simple as changing your clothes though.

Inside the chrysalis an incredible thing happens. The caterpillar turns into a butterfly! The process can take as little as two weeks or as long as several years. It all depends on the type of butterfly and how warm the temperature is outside.

19

Are you ready for Stage 4? This is the butterfly stage!

Once the butterfly emerges from its chrysalis it must wait until its wings unfold and dry before it can fly.

Did you know that butterflies do not grow? They stay the same size their entire life.

Can you remember what butterflies love to drink? Nectar is right! Some butterflies also feed on things like pollen, tree sap, rotting fruit, and dung.

Butterflies also need water, salt, and other minerals. They are just like you; your body needs these nutrients as well.

Butterfly (Adult) Stage
Monarch Butterfly

Do you know why a butterfly might land on you?

It might be attracted to the color of your clothing, or it might be attracted to the salt on your skin and clothes. When you run and play your body sweats. When your sweat dries it leaves behind salt, which is a nutrient that butterflies need.

How is a butterfly's body different from a caterpillar's body?

Butterflies have wings! They have four of them. Do you know that their wings are covered in scales? What other creatures have scales?

Butterflies can see very well, unlike caterpillars. In the chrysalis a caterpillar's eyes change from "simple" eyes into "complex" eyes. Complex eyes let butterflies see shapes and colors, both close and far away. They can see the same colors you can, and some can even see colors you can't, called ultraviolet colors.

Caterpillars chew their food with their mouth and butterflies suck nectar from flowers with their tongue-like straw, called a proboscis.

A Butterfly's Body

4 Wings
(1 forewing and 1 hindwing on each side)

Abdomen

Thorax

Head

2 Eyes
(1 on each side)

6 Legs
(3 on each side)

2 Antennae

Proboscis

Butterflies have taste buds on their proboscis, just like you have taste buds on your tongue. Do you know where else they have taste buds? Can you guess? They have taste buds on their antennae, legs and feet. If you had taste buds on the bottom of your feet what would you have tasted today?

Nature is full of funny and creative things! What's funny? Well, giant swallowtail caterpillars look pretty funny. They look like bird droppings! Isn't that funny?

Would you feel lucky if you looked like a bird dropping? No? I think giant swallowtail caterpillars feel lucky because it helps them hide from birds and animals. Bird droppings are very easy to ignore, except when they land on your head. Ick!

Having a disguise is only one of the many creative ways that caterpillars, and butterflies, are able to protect themselves.

Some are poisonous because of the food they eat, like monarch caterpillars and butterflies.

Can you think of other funny and creative ways caterpillars and butterflies protect themselves?

Did you think of these?

Some have markings, like the eyespot on the giant owl butterfly. An eyespot can make a butterfly look like a bigger, more dangerous animal.

Some have a stinky smell.

Some blend into their environment, like this caterpillar. It has the same color and stripe as the leaf. This is called camouflage.

Do you know that some butterflies can travel very long distances? This is called migration.

The most incredible migration is that of the monarch butterflies. At the very same time every year millions of them travel from Canada and the northern part of the United States, all the way down to Central Mexico. That's more than 2,000 miles!

Not all monarchs make the trip; some prefer to stay at home. They are called resident monarchs. Those that do migrate start their journey in early September of each year. They fly over water, prairies, and mountains, stopping along the way for food and rest.

U.S.A.

MEXICO

Two months later, in early November, the monarch butterflies finally arrive in Central Mexico. The skies are full of butterflies. Millions of them!

The people of Mexico celebrate their arrival. They do this because they believe that the butterflies carry the souls of their ancestors. The miracle of the monarch migration also brings many tourists from far away places.

The butterflies spend the winter in the forest, resting from their long trip. They huddle together on tree trunks and branches, under the canopy of the forest. The trees, heated by the sun during the day, keep the butterflies warm during the cold nights.

In late February, after almost five months of rest, the butterflies will start their journey home. They will travel as far north as Texas and Louisiana, where they will have children who will continue the northern journey. Those butterflies will then have children of their own, who will make the final leg of the migration. They are the grandchildren of the original butterflies that flew down to Mexico.

Then, in early September, the migration process will start all over again. A new generation of monarch butterflies will begin their trip to Mexico, just as their ancestors had done.

How do butterflies find their way to places they have never been? It is a mystery. Some think that they use the sun's position in the sky to guide them, but no one knows for sure.

Now that you have learned all about butterflies, would you like to meet some of my favorite butterfly friends?

Fido the California Dogface Sulfur

This is my friend Fido the California Dogface Sulfur. Where do you think you can find butterflies like Fido? That is a silly question, isn't it? They live in California. That's why they are called California dogface sulfurs! Fido is using his proboscis to drink nectar from a flower.

Elvis the Hawaiian Blue

My friend Elvis is a Hawaiian blue butterfly. He is only one of two types of butterflies that come from Hawaii. Elvis is smaller than most butterflies, but he is not the smallest. The western pygmy blue butterfly is the smallest butterfly in the world. It is from Africa and has a wingspan of only half an inch.

Lillian the Painted Lady

My friend, Lillian, and her family of painted lady butterflies can be seen on almost every continent and island in the world. She has a very big family! How big is your family?

Luey the Lupine Blue

If you like to hike and camp in the mountains you may have seen my friend Luey the Lupine Blue butterfly. Luey and his family of lupine blue butterflies can be found in higher altitudes, like the Pacific Coast Range and the Rocky Mountains. The next time you go camping look for Luey.

Sofia the Giant Swallowtail

My friend Sofia the Giant Swallowtail is one of the largest and most beautiful butterflies in the United States. She is big, but she is only half the size of the largest butterfly in the world. The queen alexandra birdwing butterfly from New Guinea is the largest. It is about the size of a medium pizza!

Collin the Comma butterfly gets his name from the white mark on the side of his wing. It looks like a "comma," doesn't it? My friend, Collin, is a very patient butterfly. He and other male commas like to sit in the same place for long periods of time waiting for a girlfriend to fly by.

What does the underside of Collin's wings look like?

Would you be able to see Collin if he were holding on to the bark of a tree?

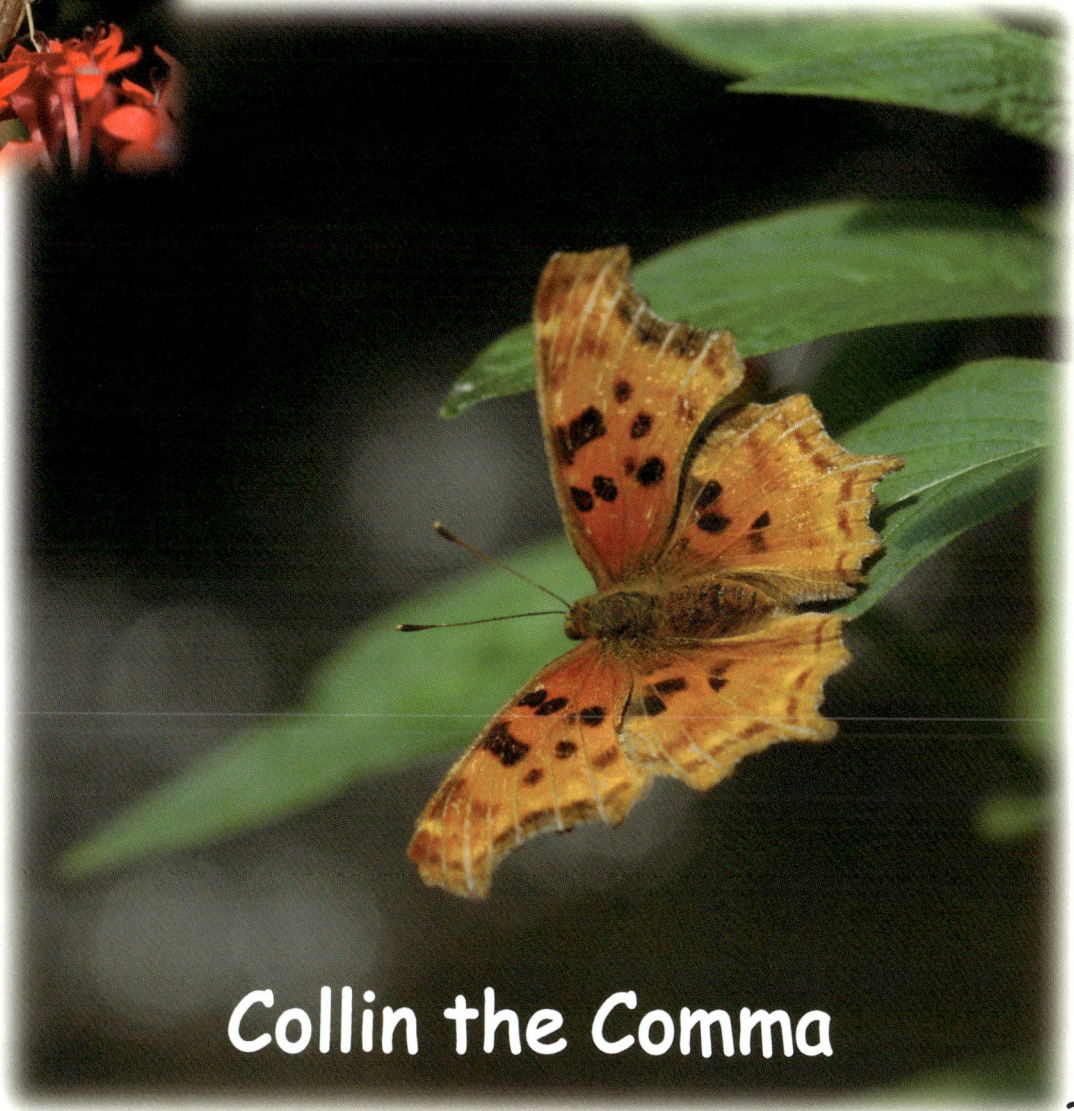

Collin the Comma

Catherine the Cabbage White

Can you count the number of spots on my friend Catherine's wings? She has two spots on each wing; that means she is a female. If she only had one spot on each wing then she would be a "he." In warmer climates my friend Catherine and her cabbage white butterfly family can be seen almost all year.

Spaz the Skipper

Do you know which butterfly is the fastest flier? It's my friend, Spaz, and his skipper butterfly family. Skippers are faster than any other type of butterfly. Spaz can fly up to 37 miles per hour. Most of the other butterflies can only fly 5 to 12 miles per hour.

Pamela the Paper Kite

My friend Pamela the Paper Kite butterfly is from Southeast Asia. Her delicate wings look like rice paper, and they are as thin as tissue paper. Pamela and my other butterfly friends are very fragile, so please do not touch them.

Freddy the Fritillary

I am so lucky to have a friend like Freddy the Fritillary butterfly. He is always doing good things for others! Do you know what makes Freddy and his family of fritillary butterflies special? They live longer than the average butterfly, and that means they are able to pollinate many more plants and flowers than most butterflies.

Gracie the West Coast Lady

This is my friend Gracie the West Coast Lady butterfly. She is very pretty! Gracie and her family can be seen from Southwestern Canada all the way down to Northern Mexico.

Moo is my Cattleheart butterfly friend. Moo can be seen in places like Mexico and Central America. Do you know that there are about 165,000 different types of butterflies in the world?

Moo the Cattleheart

Jetta the Tailed Jay

My friend Jetta loves to flutter her wings and fly high among the treetops. Jetta and her family of tailed jay butterflies live in countries like India, Singapore, and Australia. When you have friends from different places you learn a lot of fun things about their cultures and traditions. Where do your friends come from?

Julia the Orange Julia

Julia the Orange Julia butterfly, and her family of orange julias, can be seen from South Texas and Florida all the way down to Brazil. My friend Julia is fast, but she is not as fast as my friend Spaz the Skipper butterfly. **43**

This is Carly the
Monarch butterfly.

Did you see her picture in the
book, **Queen Iween's Bug Buddies**?
She was only in the caterpillar stage
at that time. Now she is a beautiful
adult monarch butterfly!

She has gone through a complete
metamorphosis. Can you remember
all the stages of a complete
metamorphosis? I know you
can. You are so smart!

Carly the Monarch butterfly

Carly the Monarch butterfly is in the final stage of her metamorphosis.

Queen Iween's Quiz

1. How do butterflies help the world and everyone in it?
    (Page 6)

2. Where is the one place in the world you cannot find butterflies?
    (Page 8)

3. How many stages are there to a complete metamorphosis?
    (Page 10)

4. What is another name for a caterpillar?
    (Page 10)

5. What keeps butterfly eggs from rolling off leaves?
    (Page 12)

6. How many times does a caterpillar shed its skin?
    (Page 18)

7. Which has better eyesight, a butterfly or a caterpillar?
    (Page 22)

8. What can a butterfly's foot do?
    (Page 23)

9. What did Sofia the Giant Swallowtail butterfly look like as a caterpillar?
    (Page 24)

10. Which one of my friends is your favorite butterfly friend? Why?

Let's play a game!

Can you find the matching pictures? There are two of each except one is missing its match.

This might be hard, but I know you can do it!

How did you do? Did you also find the one that is missing its match? Here is a hint for you:

Page 37

Would you like to
do good things to help
butterflies?

They really need your help!
Here are some ideas
for you...

5 Great Ideas For How You Can Help!

Great Idea #1

Help increase the number of host plants for butterflies.

Host plants are those plants that butterflies lay their eggs on.

Each type of butterfly has a different host plant; for example, monarch butterflies use milkweed as a host plant, and painted ladies use thistle as a host plant.

Learn more about butterflies that live in your area so that you can plant the right type of host plants.

Great Idea #2

Help provide more food for butterflies!

Put flowering plants in your garden. Butterflies like butterfly bushes, lantana, marigolds, chrysanthemums, asters and many others. Grow plants that are from your area so that they will be easier for you to take care of.

Great Idea #3

Help keep your yard safe for butterflies.

Ask your family not to use chemicals in your yard. Chemicals hurt butterflies and butterfly-friendly plants. There are natural ways of controlling pests and weeds in the yard. Help everyone be butterfly friendly.

Great Idea #4

Help butterflies live longer so they can pollinate more flowers and plants.

Please do not touch butterflies! They are very fragile and can get hurt easily.

Great Idea #5

Help spread the word!

Share what you have learned with everyone you know so they will be butterfly friendly just like you!

Thank you for stopping in to see me. I hope you had fun learning about butterflies.

Don't forget that butterflies are very important and very fragile so "Bee gentle and bee wise, only touch with your eyes." If you do not touch butterflies they will live longer and pollinate many more plants and flowers.

Glossary

Abdomen (ab-do-men)
  The rear part of the body of an insect.

Ancestor (an-ses-tor)
  A person in your family who lived a long time before you were born.

Antenna (an-ten-a)
  One of a pair of long thin body parts on the head of insects, crabs, and other animals. Depending on the animal, antenna are used to feel, smell, or taste.

Camouflage (cam-ou-flage)
  Protective coloring or covering that enables something to blend into its surroundings.

Chrysalis (kris-a-lis)
  The pupa of a butterfly that is outwardly inactive and enclosed in a firm case in which the adult butterfly eventually emerges.

Dung (duhng)
  The manure or waste of an animal.

Endoskeleton (en-doh-skel-eh-tehn)
  The internal bony framework of the body.

Exoskeleton (ek-soh-skel-eh-tehn)
  A hard outer structure that provides protection or support for an animal.

Herbivore (her-beh-vor)
  A living thing that eats only plants.

Hind Leg (hind)
  A leg at or near the rear.

Host Plant (hohst)
  A plant on which an insect lives and feeds.

Invertebrate (in-vuhr-teh-breht)
  An animal that does not have a skeleton with a backbone inside its body.

Larva (lar-va)
  An insect after it hatches from an egg and before it changes into an adult. It has no wings and looks like a worm.

Glossary continued on next page

Glossary - Page 2

Metamorphosis (meta-mor-pho-sis)
The changes in form as some things grow; a caterpillar to a butterfly and a tadpole to a frog are examples.

Migration (mi-gray-shen)
The seasonal movement of a population of animals from one area to another.

Nectar (nek-tehr)
The sweet liquid plants make that attracts birds and insects.

Pollen (pa-lehn)
The fine powder-like material made by flowering plants that helps the plant make new plants.

Pollinate (pa-lehn-ate)
To move or carry pollen from one plant or flower to another.

Proboscis (pro-bahs-kis)
The slender, tubular, feeding and sucking structure of certain invertebrates, such as insects.

Proleg (pro-leg)
One of the stubby legs on the abdomen of some insect larvae.

Pupa (pu-pah)
An insect in the stage of development between the larva and adult, during which it typically undergoes a complete change within a protective hardened case.

Shed (shed)
To cast off or molt the skin, feathers, shell, fur, or horns, and replace with new growth.

Thorax (tho-rax)
The middle part of an insect's body that is located between the head and abdomen.

Ultraviolet Color (ultra-vio-let)
A color that people cannot see, but is visible by some birds and insects. It comes after violet at the end of the visible color spectrum.

Vertebrate (vuhr-teh-brit)
An animal that has a skeleton with a backbone inside its body.

LaVergne, TN USA
15 March 2010
176036LV00001B